Lessons
and Stories *from*
Brave Little
Children

Coronavirus 2020

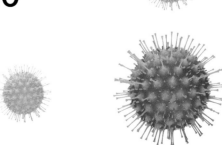

To order additional copies of this book, contact:
Xlibris
844-714-8691
www.Xlibris.com
Orders@Xlibris.com

ISBN: 978-1-6641-4031-8 (sc)
ISBN: 978-1-6641-4030-1 (e)

Print information available on the last page

Rev. date: 12/22/2020

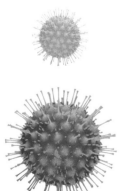

During Coronavirus 2020,
Children around the world had courage
To face pain, fear, danger, and love.

This book deals with experiences from young children.

Their firsthand experiences became life lessons and stories.

Many children around the world may have the same experiences.

Their lessons and stories may be similar in different settings.

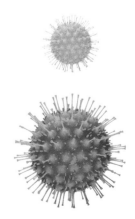

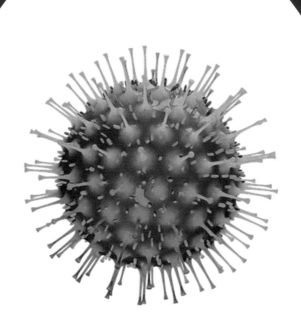

Firsthand experiences
from young children
remain with them for life.

Love me, Love you
Love all
Stay home, Wendy

dedication, and caring
for all, wash your
hands, keep your
distance, Kevin

Be Brave,
show sympathy to others
who lost love ones
Ming.
Pray for all
Thanks to all workers
Stay safe
Aadi

The year is 2020. Schools are closed all over the world.

It is not school holidays or national holidays.

They are closed because of the 2020 COVID-19 pandemic.

Children stayed at home. Some of their parents went
to work, and some worked from home.

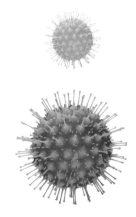

This book has four short stories that are made up of things
children did, heard, read, and were told.

They were based on firsthand experiences from children
during the 2020 COVID -19 pandemic.

They made a promise to one another to write their stories.

These stories were written on paper.

The children will take them to school and will be
shared with their teacher and classmates.

These young children were in third grade at school. They were friends.

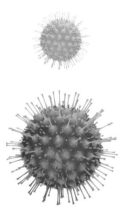

The friends were Wendy, Ming, Kevin, and Aadi.

Their parents set them up to have a one-time, thirty-minute chat. This was supervised by their parents.

This was done as a virtual conversation.

The four children ended their talk by making a promise to write their stories and take them to school when the COVID-19 pandemic is over.

They then said their goodbyes and told one another to be safe.

My name is Wendy. This is my story and the lessons I learned during Coronavirus 2020.

I am an only child. I have not seen my grandparents, my
cousins, or my friends for over a month.

Sometimes, I talked to my grandparents and cousins on the telephone.

My parents worked from home.

I noticed, they talked to their friends and other workers through their computer.

One day, I asked my parents to help me talk with my friends also.

This was done, and that was why we decided to write our little stories and lessons.

I missed my teacher, my classmates, and my friends.
I said to Ming, "Ming, I am sorry about your grandmother, take care of your grandfather."
I stayed at home while my parents worked from home.
While my parents worked, I must be quiet so I don't disturb them.

During my all alone time, I read, watched television, and most times, I looked out the window.
I spent quality times with my parents at breakfast, lunch, and dinner.
In the evenings, we watched family shows and the news on television.
Then we prayed together for everyone before going to bed.
These are my life lessons: respect all, stay home, love me, love you, love all, and prevent others from getting sick.
New words I learned are *virtual*, *virus*, *pandemic*, and names of some countries in the world.

My name is Ming.

This is my Coronavirus 2020 story.

I missed my friends, my teacher, and my school, but we must stay at home and be safe because of the Coronavirus.

I will always remember the year of the Coronavirus.

My grandma died from the Coronavirus.

We cried and cried.

We were sad.

We also cried for others who were sick and could not be with their families.

I said to my friends, "Thanks for your condolences."

My grandma loved to cook.

My grandma loved everyone.

She loved her children and
her grandchildren.

Most of all, she loved my
grandfather and carnation flowers.

Life lessons I learned are to be
brave, love all, and show sympathy
to others who lost loved ones.

New words I learned are
*mortuary, virtual viewing,
sympathy,* and *condolences.*

My name is Kevin. This is my Coronavirus 2020 story and the lessons I learned.

This is what I said to Ming, "Ming, I am sorry to hear about
your loss, my condolences to you and your love ones."

My mother is a nurse, and she works all the time.
We are scared when she goes to work.
We told her to stay home because we do not want to lose her.
My mother said, she must go every day to help the sick people and sick children.

I also stayed home with my dad, a younger brother, and a baby sister.
I am also a small child, but I help my dad with caring for my siblings.

My mother has a picture of a lamp with an important nurse named
Florence Nightingale.
She is also called the Lady with the lamp.
She is my mother's heroine.

My life lessons are dedication, hard work, and caring for others.
Some new words I learned are *hero* and *heroine*, *essential workers*
and *front-line workers*, and *scientist*.

My name is Aadi. This is my Coronavirus 2020 story and the life lessons I learned.

I said to Ming, "Ming, I am sorry to hear about your loss,
my hand is holding your hand from a distance."

I missed school, my teacher, and my friends.

My dad had Coronavirus and was in the hospital for ten days.

We were scared and sad.

My mother, my sister, and I did not go to see him at the hospital.

The virus was contagious.

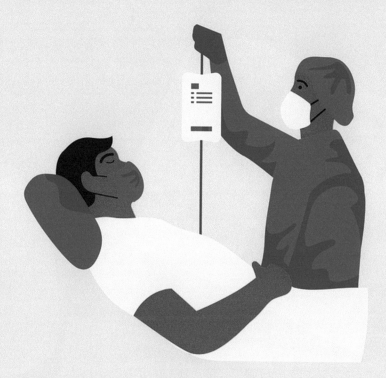

The nurses and doctors took care of my dad.
He got better while he recovered at home after he was discharged from the hospital.
We are lucky my dad lived, and we are happy to have him home again.
We hope and pray the virus will go away and there would be a vaccine for this virus.
Life lessons I learned are, always to thank front-line workers, first responders, essential workers, nurses, and doctors.

Pray for all, and stay safe.
Keep your distance

New words I learned are *contagious*, *transmission*, *positive*, *negative*, *ventilator*, and *isolation*.

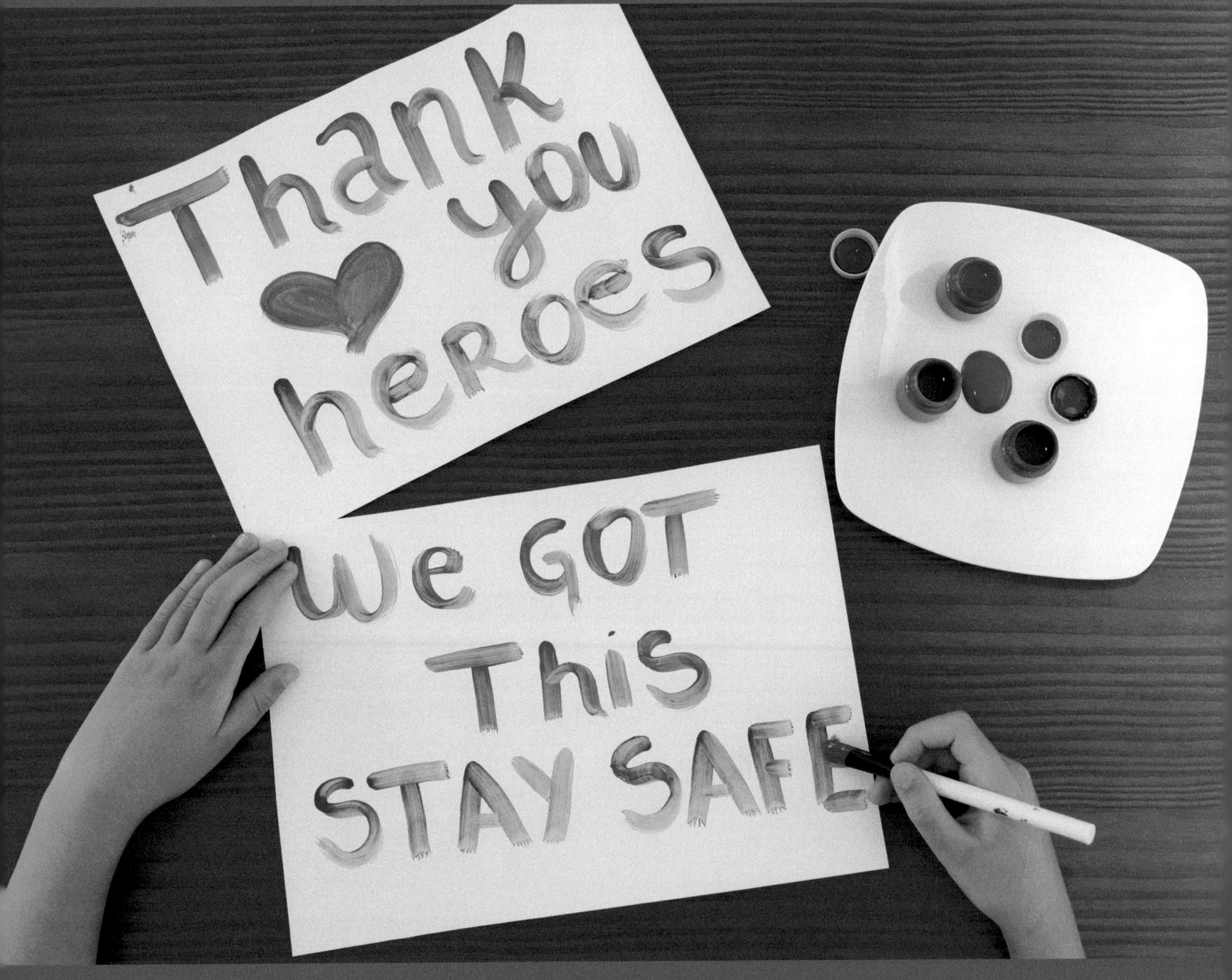
Thank you heroes
We GOT This
STAY SAFE

From Wendy, Ming, Kevin, Aadi, and all the children of the world.

Thanks to all the courageous people who are frontline workers, essential workers, and all other workers who helped during Coronavirus 2020.

You are brave and beautiful.

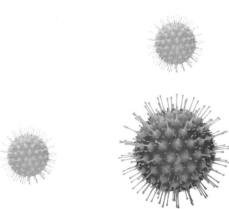

From the children in my book and me

Thanks to the doctors, nurses, and other medical workers for their services during the 2020 COVID-19 pandemic.

Printed in the United States
By Bookmasters